To the reader:

Welcome to the DK ELT Graded R
different. They explore aspects of th
history, geography, science … and a lot of other things. And
they show the different ways in which people live now, and
lived in the past.

These DK ELT Graded Readers give you material for
reading for information, and reading for pleasure. You are
using your English to do something real. The illustrations
will help you understand the text, and also help bring the
Reader to life. Listen to the cassette or CD as well, and you
can really enter the world of the Olympic Games, the
Titanic, or the Trojan War … and a lot more. Choose the
topics that interest you, improve your English, and learn
something … all at the same time.
Enjoy the series!

To the teacher:

This series provides varied reading practice at five levels of
language difficulty, from elementary to FCE level:
BEGINNER
ELEMENTARY A
ELEMENTARY B
INTERMEDIATE
UPPER INTERMEDIATE
The language syllabus has been designed to suit the factual
nature of the series, and includes a wider vocabulary range
than is usual with ELT readers: language linked with the
specific theme of each book is included and glossed. The
language scheme, and ideas for exploiting the material
(including the recorded material) both in and out
of class are contained in the Teacher's Resource
Book. We hope you and your students enjoy
using this series.

A DORLING KINDERSLEY BOOK

DK www.dk.com

Originally published as Eyewitness Reader
Dinosaur Dinners in 1998 and adapted as an
ELT Graded Reader for
Dorling Kindersley by

studio cactus C

13 SOUTHGATE STREET WINCHESTER HAMPSHIRE SO23 9DZ

Published in Great Britain by
Dorling Kindersley Limited
9 Henrietta Street, London WC2E 8PS

2 4 6 8 10 9 7 5 3 1

Copyright © 2000
Dorling Kindersley Limited, London

A CIP catalogue record for this book is
available from the British Library.

ISBN 0-7513-3167-8

Colour reproduction by Colourscan, Singapore
Printed and bound in China by L. Rex Printing Co., Ltd
Text film output by Ocean Colour, UK

The publisher would like to thank the following:
Museums: Natural History Museum, London, and
Royal Tyrrel Museum of Palaeontology, Alberta

Artists/model makers: Roby Braun, Jim Channell, John
Holmes, Graham High/Jeremy Hunt/Centaur Studios, and
Kenneth Lilly

Photographers: Andy Crawford, John Downs,
Neil Fletcher, Dave King, Tim Ridley, and Dave Rudkin
Jacket credit: The Natural History Museum, London

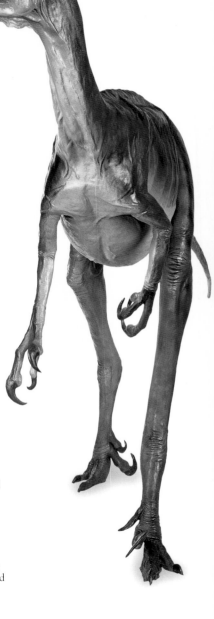

ELT Graded Readers

ELEMENTARY A

DINOSAURS

Written by
Caroline Laidlaw
Series Editor Susan Holden

London • New York • Delhi • Sydney

Dinosaurs were reptiles that lived between 230 million and 65 million years ago. They are extinct now. Their closest relatives, crocodiles and birds, are still living in the world today.

The word "dinosaur" comes from two Greek words: deinos "terrible" and sauros "lizard".

This dinosaur is *Troodon*. Its name means "wounding tooth", because it had teeth like sharp knives that could easily wound and kill.

Troodon lived about 76–70 million years ago. It was about the same size as a human being. Scientists think it was one of the most intelligent dinosaurs, because it had quite a large brain. It also had very good eyesight and was a fast runner.

A dangerous dinosaur
Troodon could run very fast. It was a clever hunter. It could see animals even in bad light, because it had good eyesight. Nothing could hide from this dinosaur.

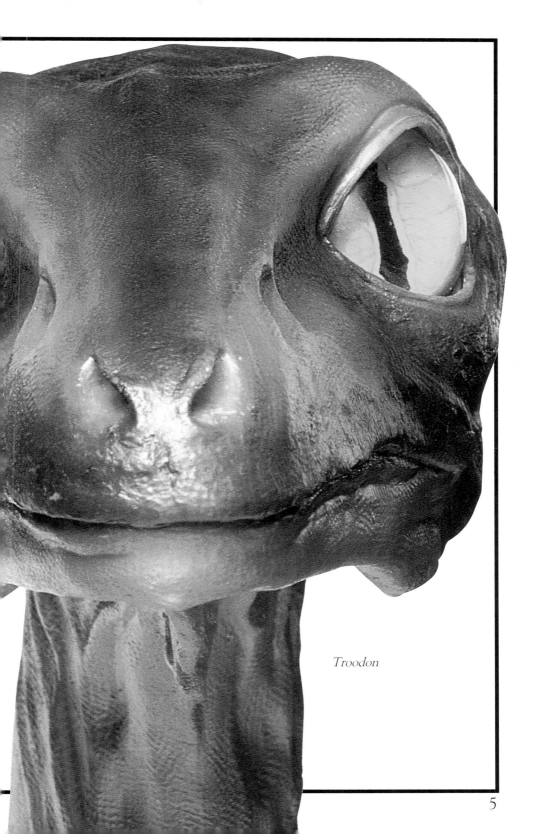

Troodon

5

This dinosaur is *Herrerasaurus*. A man called Victorino Herrera discovered its bones in Argentina in 1958. It lived about 228 million years ago. It was about 3–4 metres long and had strong back legs, a short neck, and a big head. It could run very fast on its two back legs. It was also a good hunter, like *Troodon*.

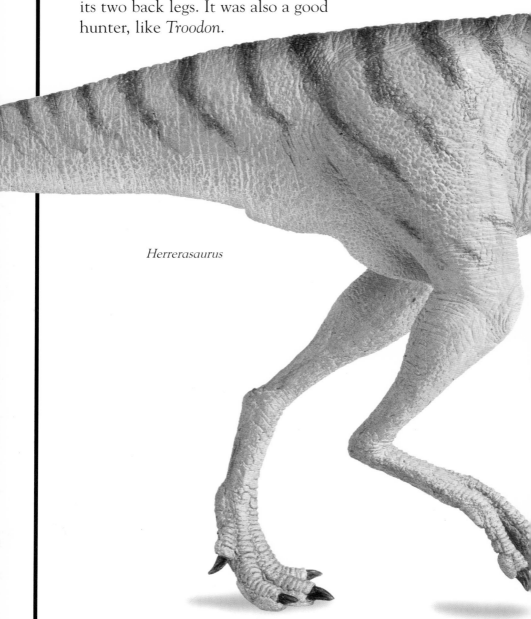

Herrerasaurus

Where did *Troodon* and *Herrerasaurus* find food?

They found it behind rocks and under leaves. These were the hiding places of small snakes and lizards. But before they could catch their food, the dinosaurs had to run very fast. The snakes and lizards could also move quickly. They could run away.

A fast runner
Herrerasaurus had strong back legs. It could run very fast. It liked eating small reptiles, like snakes and lizards.

Tyrannosaurus rex was a fierce predator. It was about 12 metres long, and 20 metres tall. Its head was huge, and it had more than 60 strong teeth. Each tooth was 23 centimetres long. It could eat 230 kilos of meat and bones in one bite!

Tyrannosaurus rex lived 67–65 million years ago. It became extinct about 65 million years ago. Many other dinosaurs also died. Scientists are not sure why. Perhaps a giant meteorite hit the Earth and caused a change of climate. It became very cold and dinosaurs couldn't find food.

A huge hunter
Tyrannosaurus liked eating animals for its dinner. Its name means "tyrant lizard". It was one of the biggest meat-eaters in the world of dinosaurs.

Tyrannosaurus

What kind of food did these three dinosaurs eat? You can find the answer in their teeth, claws, and legs. Only the meat-eaters had sharp teeth and claws like these. And they had strong back legs because they were hunters and had to catch their prey. Animals that hunt other animals are called predators. The hunted animals are called prey.

Tyrannosaurus

Troodon

Herrerasaurus

Hungry for meat
These dinosaurs were carnivores,
or meat-eaters. They only ate
meat. Their favourite food was
fish, insects, and small animals
including other dinosaurs.

In the 1970s, scientists found the fossil bones of this dinosaur in the Gobi desert (China). Its name is *Gallimimus* which means "acting like a chicken".

In fact, it looked more like an ostrich but it didn't have wings. It had a beak, a small head, a long neck, a long tail, short arms, and hollow bones. It was one of the most intelligent dinosaurs. It had a good brain in its small head! And its hollow bones were very useful. It was not heavy like many of the other big dinosaurs.

Gallimimus

Animals and plants: a mixed diet
Gallimimus had a long beak, like a bird. It could pick up leaves, and it could catch small animals in its beak. It was an omnivore.

Gallimimus was an omnivore. This means it had a mixed diet of plants and meat. It liked eating eggs, too. *Gallimimus* lived about 75–70 million years ago. It was about 5–6 metres long, but it wasn't heavy because it had hollow bones. Sometimes big meat-eating dinosaurs tried to catch it for food. Usually, it could escape. With its hollow bones it was light and could run very fast on its two back legs. It could reach a speed of about 70 kilometres an hour.

About 80–65 million years ago, North America was the home of a plant-eating dinosaur called *Maiasaura*. It was unusual because it made nests and looked after its babies. The name *Maiasaura* means "good mother lizard".

In Montana (USA) scientists found about 10,000 Maiasaura fossils in a huge group. The dinosaurs probably lived in herds. It is possible that they moved together from place to place, looking for fresh plant food.

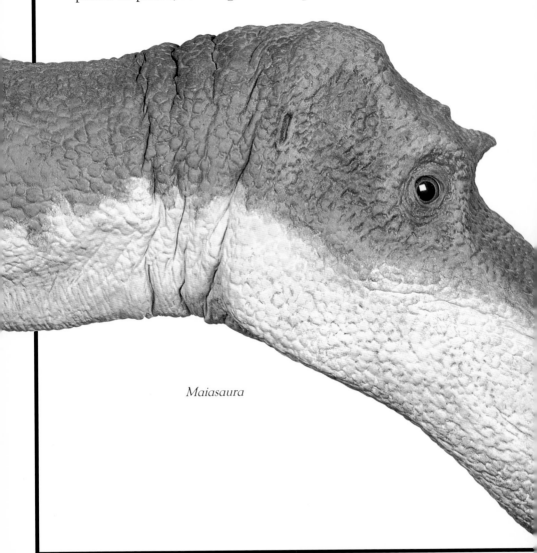

Maiasaura

Eggs in a nest
Maiasaura made nests in the ground. Their babies came out of eggs, like baby birds and crocodiles.

First, the female *Maiasaura* made a nest. It was a simple hole in the ground, 1.8–2 metres wide. Then she laid her eggs. She laid a lot of eggs. But she didn't leave the nest. Instead, she stayed near it and guarded her eggs. Later, she looked after her new babies. She was a very good mother. It was hard work because they were always hungry. Like their mother, they ate leaves, berries, and seeds. They were vegetarians.

Herbivore dinosaurs had a problem: the carnivores liked eating them because they were very tasty. But what could the herbivores do about it? Well, there were several answers. For example, some of them developed very thick skin. They also had horns and spikes on their heads and bodies. They looked like warriors ready for battle in a suit of armour. So they were not easy prey for the carnivores.

   Styracosaurus had spikes on its head, and a horn on its nose. Its name means "spiked lizard". It was about 5 metres long and about 1.8 metres tall. It lived 77–70 million years ago. It walked on four short legs and could reach a speed of 32 kilometres an hour.

Strong armour

Styracosaurus had a long horn on its nose. It used the horn for protection. Of course, the rhinoceros of today isn't a dinosaur, but it has a horn on its nose, just like *Styracosaurus*.

Styracosaurus

Edmontosaurus means "lizard from Edmonton", which is in Canada. They lived in this region.

It is another example of a dinosaur with a protective skin. It was about 13 metres long and was extremely heavy. It could run on two legs, or walk on four. But it was not a fast mover. Scientists think that it probably had good senses (eyesight, hearing, and smell). These senses warned *Edmontosaurus* of predators nearby. It hid from them in swamps because it couldn't run fast.

There are thousands of *Edmontosaurus* fossils in Alberta, Canada. They lived there in herds 73–65 million years ago. But scientists believe that every winter they left the far north because it was dark and there was no food. They travelled thousands of kilometres to Alberta, which had a lot of green plants during winter. These dinosaurs were migratory. They moved with the weather, away from the cold weather. A lot of birds and animals today are migratory. Do you know any in your country?

Edmontosaurus

Meet *Euoplocephalus*, a plant-eating dinosaur that lived 70–65 million years ago. In the early 1900s, scientists found more than 40 fossils of this huge animal in Alberta (Canada) and Montana (USA).

With four short legs and a very short neck, *Euoplocephalus* could only eat plants near the ground. And because its legs were short and its body was so heavy, it could not move fast. Even worse, it was not very clever.

Big dinosaurs often made good meals for other dinosaurs! How, then, did *Euoplocephalus* escape from predators?

Well, we know that it had very thick skin and its head was well-armoured. The big meat-eating dinosaurs could not easily attack it. There was only one part of its body that was soft – its belly. A clever predator could turn *Euoplocephalus* onto its back, and then kill it. Scientists believe it was probably the favourite meal of *Tyrannosaurus rex*.

The name *Euoplocephalus* means "well-armoured head".

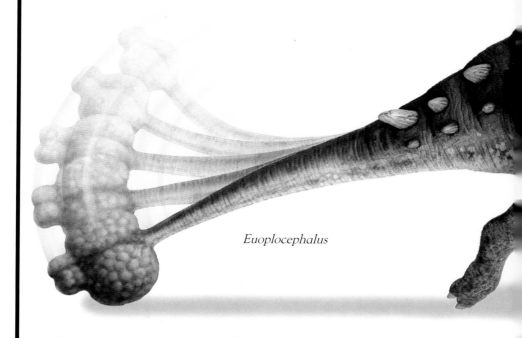

Euoplocephalus

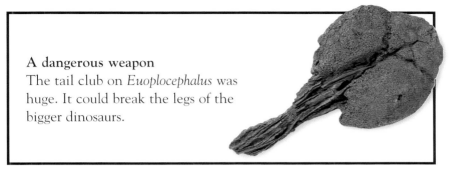

A dangerous weapon
The tail club on *Euoplocephalus* was huge. It could break the legs of the bigger dinosaurs.

Like *Edmontosaurus*, it was a dinosaur with a very thick skin. It had a wide head with a beak and horns. On its body there were hard plates and spikes. On the end of its tail there was a heavy club, which could break the legs of bigger dinosaurs. It was about 6 metres long and weighed about 2 tons. It looked fierce!

Hypsilophodon was one of the smallest herbivores. It was about 2 metres long and about 60 centimetres tall. It weighed about 68 kilos. It ate plants that grew on the ground, like grass. So, like many herbivores, it tasted good!

It didn't have any spikes or horns for protection. So, how did it fight the meat-eaters? The answer is that it didn't fight, it ran. And it could run very fast indeed on its strong back legs. It could run faster than the big dinosaurs.

Perhaps it is sometimes better to run away, and not to fight!

This little dinosaur probably lived in a herd with other *Hypsilophodons*. This was a good idea because, in a group, there were many eyes watching out for enemies. They probably also looked after their nests and babies.

Scientists found a group of 20 fossils on the Isle of Wight (an island off the coast of southern England). *Hypsilophodon* lived 120 million years ago.

Hypsilophodon was a small dinosaur, but it could look after itself!

Hypsilophodon

Corythosaurus was a herbivore with a kind of helmet on its head. Its name means "helmet lizard" but the helmet didn't protect the animal. In fact, *Corythosaurus* didn't have any kind of natural protection. It wasn't like the other plant-eating dinosaurs that had armoured bodies. But it could run fast, and it probably had a good sense of smell. Running away was a good protection against its enemies. Many of the big dinosaurs were very heavy and slow, and could not run fast.

Corythosaurus lived 80–65 million years ago. In 1914, Barnum Brown found the first fossil in Alberta (Canada). Later, scientists found more *Corythosaurus* fossils in other parts of North America.

Corythosaurus

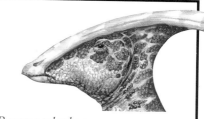

Parasaurolophus

Why did *Corythosaurus* have a "helmet", or crest, on its head?
Scientists don't know exactly, but they have some ideas.
Firstly, perhaps the crest made a sound. Maybe *Corythosaurus*
could communicate with it. Secondly, perhaps the crest was a
cooling device in hot weather. Lastly, perhaps it was a kind of
nose, with a very good sense of smell. Nobody knows the
answer. What do you think?

Barosaurus means "heavy lizard", which is a very good name for one of the biggest and tallest herbivores. It probably weighed about 40,000 kilos.

A heavy dinosaur like this needed a lot of food. With its long neck, it could reach branches of trees. It probably ate the leaves of several trees in one day. It had to find places with lots of trees.

Barosaurus had short legs and walked slowly. It couldn't turn round quickly because it was very long – about 25 metres! It lived in North America and East Africa about 150 million years ago.

Barosaurus

Luckily, *Barosaurus* was taller than all the meat-eaters. It usually escaped from its enemies because it could see them from a great distance. Perhaps the big carnivores were afraid of it because it was so big, but it was really a peaceful dinosaur. It didn't like fighting.

The enemies of herbivores were meat-eaters with sharp teeth and claws. The plant-eaters didn't have sharp teeth and claws to fight with. They had tail-clubs and horns, for example, and very thick skin.

What else did they have? The pictures will remind you.

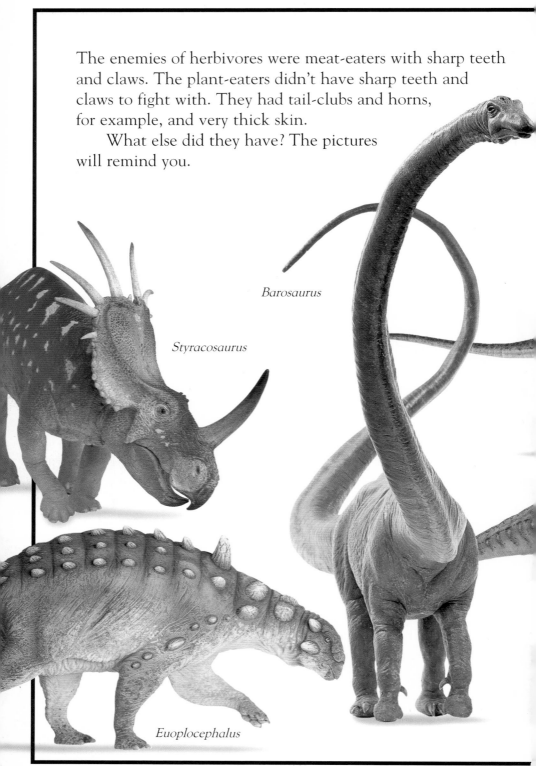

Barosaurus

Styracosaurus

Euoplocephalus

Plant lovers

Most of the dinosaurs were herbivores. At the time of dinosaurs there was a lot of food for plant-eaters. There were huge forests and many different kinds of plants.

Hypsilophodon

Edmontosaurus

Corythosaurus

Maiasaura

Here are five dinosaurs. Can you remember their names?
Which was an omnivore?
How many are herbivores?
Which was the fastest runner?
Which was the most dangerous carnivore?
Which herbivore had the longest neck?
Which dinosaur had a soft belly,
but a well-armoured back?